THE DYNAMICS AND CHALLENGES OF BLENDED FAMILIES

DR. JOHN DAVIS

TABLE OF CONTENTS

DEDICATIONS

This book is dedicated to my Lord and Savior Jesus Christ for giving me the ability to hear His voice and share His word to the world. I thank Him for the ability to inspire others in a clear, practical and relevant manner.

Secondly, I dedicate this book to my wife, Gail Davis, for pushing me to complete this book and share the Dynamics of Blended Families. Thank you for your love, and support, and for being my partner for life. We are co-parents of a blended family, and our love and appreciation extends to each of them, for their support.

To my family, friends, and the Bethesda Theological Seminary - Thank you for believing in me and constantly pushing me.

Blessings! I love all of you!

FOREWORD

By Andre' C. Barnes, SR

If there's ever been a need for real, relevant, and required ministry, it's now. There are many areas of this thing called life that require a Word from the Lord. On this high-demand subject, the Rev. Dr. John Davis has taken on the task of addressing the Dynamics and Challenges of the Blended Family experience. Note: blended families are the results of sin and the breakdown of the original intent of God. The altering of the original intent concerning the family requires a level of grace, understanding, teaching, and obedience in those seeking to honor God in their family life.

In a time when right is called wrong, wrong is called right, up is called down and down is called up, and the attacks on the nuclear family from every angle, there's a fight to maintain and even to regain the family structure: the subject of the 'Blended Family' is most needed.

Navigating the needs and required ministry of the Blended Family requires a level of love and understanding, and experience. There's a healing that has to take place because of divorce or the absent father or mother effect. Healing in understanding that though broken the family structure can be mended and restored through the love of Jesus Christ.

Dr. John Davis's experiences and knowledge of God's Word at the foundational level will provide a level of hope and instructions to those seeking God's Word on the subject matter, and serve as a great tool of healing, restoration, comfort, and repair.

Prepare your mind and heart to be encouraged, challenged, and taught in the Word of God concerning one of the most needed subject matters of our day…Families can blend, and be restored! Enjoy!

Andre' C. Barnes, SR

Author of "Crippled, But I've Got a Right to Be Here!" *Anointed Insight into the Crisis of this Current Culture* & "Can't Go Back, Can't Stay Here, What's Up Over There?" *The Changing Face of Leadership in The Body of Christ.*

www.imjustsayingdre.com

PREFACE
By Dr. Marie Burkins

As a former student of Dr. John Davis, I've come to learn that he is a man who truly cares about the welfare of the family. He is very transparent with his life experiences, and from those experiences comes the heart of a man who desires to give biblical insight into what a Godly family should look like. In a world that has a nonchalant attitude about the importance of a family union, Dr. Davis lets you see that the value of the family is the basis for social order. Even in the midst of discord and conflict we see in so many of today's families, he will inform you on how you can personally bring structure, comfort, love, and respect to your relationships.

"The Dynamics and Challenges of Blended Families" is a must-read for anyone who is confronted with the newness of bringing two families together, to make a life together with the children from one or both previous relationships. The process of forming a new, blended family can be challenging, but it can also be rewarding. Using the Word of God as his foundation, Dr. John Davis will show you that joy can come from the difficulties faced with the new

relationships. He will show that you can feel secure even when you may feel, at times, to be vulnerable.

"The Dynamics and Challenges of Blended Families" can be used as a guide to show God's grace and healing in new relationships, where every person is a special individual but they are also united as one, affectionately connected to one another to bring peace, love, and harmony to the family and, ultimately, to their society.

Dr. Marie Burkins

Bethesda Theological Seminary

CHAPTER ONE

GOD'S ORIGINAL CREATION AND PURPOSE FOR MARRIAGE AND THE FAMILY

It is important to first understand God's original purpose for marriage and the family. Marriage and the family are not an invention of man, neither was it an afterthought by God, but the family was a part of God's original six-day creation.

The family was the first institution that God created in the earth. It was created and designed to reproduce the image and glory of God in the earth, through the human family.

Therefore, the first blessing and commandment that God gave to mankind were, to reproduce themselves. *"Be fruitful and multiply"*, to have sex, and reproduce themselves through children.

> ***Genesis 1:26-28*** *And God said, Let us make man in our image, after our likeness: So God created man in **his own image,** in the **image of God** created he him; **male** and **female** created he them. And God blessed them, and God said unto them, **Be fruitful,***

> ***and multiply***, *and* ***replenish the earth,*** *and subdue it.*

Because God creates by the power of the spoken word, this spoken word of blessing, and commandment by God, created and brought into existence, the physical and biological design of the man and the woman, to do what He commanded them to do. Therefore, children are the heritage and reward of God Himself!

> ***Psalm 127:3-5*** *Lo, children are an heritage of the LORD: and the fruit of the womb is his reward. As arrows are in the hand of a mighty man; so are children of the youth. Happy is the man that hath his quiver full of them.*

Therefore, man, woman, and the family were created by God for the purpose of reproducing, and developing the human race, through a covenant relationship of marriage, and a binding love of affection and care, which is a reflection of the image, love, and glory of God in the earth.

Therefore, according to the creative law of God, human sexuality, and reproduction, were limited to the covenant of marriage; therefore, blended families were never a part of God's original plan and purpose for the family.

> *Genesis 2:24 Therefore shall a **man** leave his father and his mother, and shall cleave unto his **wife**: (woman) **and they shall be one flesh.***

What God is saying here by, *"they shall be one flesh"* is that only they who are united as one in the covenant of marriage, can righteously become united as one flesh physically, and reproduce children, which is one person that comes from the two of them.

Apostle Paul clarified this for us in First Corinthians.

> *I Corinthians 6:16 What? know ye not that he which is joined to an harlot is one body? **for two, saith he, shall be one flesh.***

> *Genesis 4:1 And **Adam knew Eve his wife;** and she conceived, and bare Cain, and said, I have gotten a man from the Lord.*

Notice that the scripture says that Adam knew his wife, not his girlfriend, his significant other, his fiancée, etc. but his wife. Therefore, the scripture says:

> *Hebrews 13:4 Marriage is honourable in all, and the bed undefiled: but whoremongers and adulterers God will judge.*

Therefore, the covenant of marriage is the foundation upon which the family, society, government, and the world are built; and as the family goes, so goes society, and the world.

Because anything other than God's divine order will result in disorder, dysfunction, chaos, difficulty, stress, and excessive and unproductive labor.

> ***Psalm 127:1-2*** *Except the* Lord *build the house, they labour in vain that build it.*

What Is Vain Labor?

Vain labor is when you work hard and long hours that result in very little, fruitless, and pointless effort. It means consuming much but still not being satisfied.

To plant fields, but not receive a harvest; to build a home, but not be able to live in it. To earn wages, only to have it wasted, to put in a great effort, but see very little result.

> ***Haggai 1:6*** *Ye have sown much, and bring in little; ye eat, but ye have not enough; ye drink, but ye are not filled with drink; ye clothe you, but there is none warm; and he that earneth wages, earneth wages to put it into a bag with holes.*

This Is Why God Hates Divorce

*Malachi 2:13-15 Yet ye say, Why? Because the LORD hath been witness between thee and the **wife of thy youth**, against whom thou **hast dealt treacherously**: yet is she thy companion, and the **wife of thy covenant**. And did not he make one? Yet had he the residue of the spirit. **And why one? That he might seek a godly seed.** Therefore take heed to your spirit, and let none deal treacherously against the wife of his youth.*

*Malachi 2:16 For the LORD, the God of Israel, saith **that he hateth putting away**: for one covereth violence with his garment, saith the LORD of hosts: therefore take heed to your spirit, that ye deal not treacherously.*

God hates divorce because of what happens to the family and to every aspect of society. And because it always involves sin, unfaithfulness, and breaking the solemn oaths, and covenant vows, entered into in the presence of The Almighty God Himself.

We must understand also that a divorce is not just the husband and wife, but the entire family, bringing harmful effects and consequences, not only to the couple, but also to their children, other family members, society, and most importantly, to the image of God.

The Negative Effects Of Divorce On Children And Ways To Help Them

Divorce could be one of the most challenging phases in one's life as it involves bringing an end to the marriage. However, the negative effect of divorce on children is known to be hard.

A study reveals that in the US, the daughters of divorced parents have a higher divorce rate of 60% than 35% for sons.

However, even after divorce, you can work with your better half to ensure that the end of your marriage does not impact your children. Sometimes, parents might not know the after-effects of divorce on their child's development!

It is essential for couples to consider and discuss the potential effects of divorce on the long-term mental and physical health of their children.

In this post, we acquaint you with the challenges children might face when their parents decide to get divorced. We also suggest some ways to mitigate these negative effects and help children cope with the situation.

The Short-Term Effects Of Divorce On Children

When parents behave immaturely during a divorce and try to one-up each other, children who witness a contentious relationship between their parents may sometimes have the following short-term effects.

Anxiety: The aftermath of a divorce causes the child to become tense, nervous, and anxious. Young children are more prone to it than older ones since they are heavily dependent on both parents. An anxious child will find it difficult to concentrate on his studies and may lose interest in activities that he once found enticing.

Constant stress: According to the American Academy of Child & Adolescent Psychiatry, many children falsely consider themselves the reason behind their parents' divorce **and assume the responsibility to mend the relationship**. This can lead to immense stress and pressure on the young mind, which can have several repercussions like negative thoughts and nightmares.

Mood Swings and Irritability: Young children may suffer from mood swings and become irritable even when interacting with familiar people. Some children will go into withdrawal mode, where they stop talking to anyone and shut themselves away. The child will become quiet and prefer spending time alone.

Intense Sadness: Divorce may push children into depression and sadness.

Disillusion and Distress: Children of divorce may feel hopeless and disillusioned because they do not have the emotional support and security that they need from their parents. And this situation can worsen if the child is raised in a single-parent household with little or no access to the other parent. Short-term effects of divorce can also hamper a child's psychological, and physiological growth, which can have a long-term effect.

Long-Term Effects Of Divorce On Children

Things can get rough for a child, who sees his parents bicker and separate. Their minds are still plastic, that is they can easily get affected by the events happening around them. The following are the long-term effects of divorce on children:

Behavioral And Social Problems: A child is at greater risk of developing violent and antisocial behavior when the parents divorce. He or she may become very short-tempered, showing no hesitation in assaulting someone. This may also lead to the development of a criminal mindset, especially during the adolescent years.

Studies show that most children of divorce display the characteristic traits of aggression and disobedience with varying degrees of intensity. Extreme cases of these conditions make the child a social misfit.

Trouble With Relationships: When children grow up seeing a marriage fail, they develop doubts about love and harmony in a relationship. They may have trust and attachment issues and find it challenging to resolve conflicts in any interpersonal relationships. Such children, as adults, will start any relationship with a negative mindset. Parental alienation can also make social adjustment difficult for the child.

Prone to Substance Abuse: Drugs and alcohol become the avenue for adolescents to vent out their frustration and anxiety. Research Has Shown a Higher Incidence of Substance Abuse in Teens Whose Parents are Divorced.

Of course, there are other factors like the care provided by the single parent, which determines the adolescent's tendency to have drugs. However, the probability of an adolescent succumbing to this temptation is considerably high. Long-term substance abuse has damaging effects on the well-being of the child.

Depression: The feeling of anguish and heartbreak caused by parents' divorce can make a child slip into depression.

Depression is a mental health problem, and children who witness divorce have a higher incidence of depression, social withdrawal, and self-esteem issues. Researchers note that divorce can be a contributing factor in cases of bipolar disorder observed in children.

Poor Education And Socio-economic Position: The adverse psychological impacts of divorce diminish a child's interest in education. Children who experience divorce of their parents show a drastic drop in their school grades.

It can significantly impede a child's ability to learn at school and college. Stunted progress in education hampers the career prospects of the child as an adult, which makes it difficult to elude economic hardships in the future.

Divorce can take a toll on the children's mental and physical health, but sometimes, separated parents are far better than constant quarreling and abusive parents. Don't be surprised.

CHAPTER TWO

STATISTICS ON THE STATE OF THE FAMILY IN AMERICA TODAY

Statistics are Staggering: Studies found that the majority of families have shifted from the original biologically bonded mother, father, and child. But we are now a nation in which the majority of families are divorced. And most of them go on to remarry or form living together relationships.

These Families Take a Multitude of Forms, Such As:

- Divorced with children, and the children residing with one parent and visiting the other. And most divorcees are dating or looking for new partners.

- Remarried, re-coupled, living together, with his and/or her children; He/she is in the role of stepparent.

- Single Mothers; re-coupled, dating, and alone.

- Divorced Dads: These dads generally visit their children. Often, they are re-coupled, bringing a stepmother figure into their children's lives.

- Lesbian and gay couples: with children from a prior relationship.

According To The US Bureau of Census:

- Nearly 55% of all first marriages end in divorce.

- Nearly 60% of second marriages end in divorce.

- And Nearly 73% of third marriages end in divorce.

- About 45% of women and 50% of men will re-marry within 5 years

- About 50% of re-marriages involve children under the age of eighteen from previous marriages or relationships.

- Over 2000 blended families are started every day in America.

- About 42% of adults are in a step-relationship. This is either a step/parent, a step or half-sibling, or a stepchild. This translates to about 95.5 million adults.

- There are 16.5 million step/dads in America.

- There are 14 million step/moms in America.

- And with over 40% of all births, being to unmarried or never married women; Experts predict that blended/step/families will become the most common type of families in America.

Given these statistics, especially among some groups, there is about an 85% chance that anyone getting married today will be in a blended family. These conditions concerning the family structure are too serious to be ignored by society, especially by the church.

Now, The Dynamics And Challenges of Blended Families

A successful blended/stepfamily can be very difficult, but not impossible. Blended families have two extra stressors, however, that God never intended in His original family plan. **First**, there is someone else's ex. **Second**, there are someone else's children; thus, causing stress in blended families to increase exponentially.

Parenting is never easy, but when you have a blended family—with bio-children, stepchildren, bio-parents, stepparents, your ex, your spouse's ex, plus, other extended family members thrown into the mix; bio-grandparents, step-grandparents, and ex-grandparents, bio and step aunts, uncles, and cousins Etc.

Things can get very difficult, very quickly. Some studies show that roughly 74% of these marriages fail because of too much pressure and stress.

Other Factors That Can Challenge The Success of Blended Families

Because, break-ups and divorce, are the death of a covenant relationship with a family; and means that something that was once fulfilling and precious to everyone involved has now been broken, torn apart, and lost.

Therefore, blended families are born out of brokenness, loss, failure, hurt, grief, and bitterness. And everyone in this new family is in need of love, comfort, and healing.

This also means that everyone in a blended family has a previous relationship and history with someone else, having an ingrained living pattern, and has developed a built-in value system of living.

One of the great challenges is, the parent/child bonding relationships of the bio-parents, pre-date the current marriage. And the parent and children from a previous marriage or relationship, have already formed a living system without the new spouse.

In many cases, there is little time for the new couple to bond with each other before they are thrown into the complex role of parenting someone else's children.

And to add to those problems, in many cases, the finances in the home of blended families may be going to more than one family, for child support and other things.

And in many cases, the individuals, in blended families, do not have the conflict resolution, and communication skills themselves to solve these family problems.

As we can see then, blended families are generally made up of people who have already walked away from, and/or given up on one or more previous relationships, demonstrating their inability, or unwillingness, to deal with conflicts, and to resolve issues.

So, we see then, why these marriages can be so difficult, complex, complicated, dysfunctional, and stressful. But they can survive if they put their marriage in the hands of God and develop the skills necessary to make the marriage.

However, as difficult as these Families are, their relationship with God can remain intact, and it must if they are going to survive these marriages!

There Are Several Blended Families in The Bible That We Can Glean From

We will consider three blended families found in the Bible that mirror more closely to our blended families today.

1. Abraham had a blended family: He had Sarah his wife, and her son Isaac, and his baby momma, Hagar, and her son Ishmael. Things got so bad in his family that, Abraham had to put Hagar and his son Ishmael out of the house, causing him and them a lot of stress, grief, and suffering. **(Genesis 21)**

2. Jacob had a blended family: He had two wives, two baby mommas, and 13 children between the four of them, with disastrous results. Wives were jealous of wives, and baby mommas, and baby mommas were jealous of wives and one another. And one of Jacob's sons slept with one of his wives.

Jacob's family was torn apart by jealousy, incest, murder, deceit, and favoritism; with parents favoring one child over another, and making it obviously known; causing division, fighting, heartaches, and extreme suffering throughout his family. **(Genesis Chapters 29-38)**

3. King David had a blended family. He had many wives and baby mommas. Among his children was incest; half-brother raping half-sister, half-bothers killing half-brothers, and one son sleeping with his father's wives. The family rebellion, hatred, bitterness, and anger against siblings, and parents caused David many years of suffering, agony, frustration, and pain for everyone.

***2 Samuel 12:10** Now therefore the sword shall never depart from thine house; because thou hast despised me, and hast taken the wife of Uriah the Hittite to be thy wife.*

2 Samuel 16:21-22** And Ahithophel said unto Absalom, Go in unto thy father's concubines, which he hath left to keep the house; and all Israel shall hear that thou art abhorred of thy father: then shall the hands of all that are with thee be strong. So they spread Absalom a tent upon the top of the house; and Absalom went in unto his father's concubines in the sight of all Israel. **(Please Read 2 Samuel 13:7-30)

***Romans 15:4** For whatsoever things were written aforetime were written for our learning, that we through patience and comfort of the scriptures might have hope.*

God deliberately put these families and others in the scriptures for our example, to help us to understand what we can expect in a blended family. But in spite, of their struggles, they were able to maintain their relationship with God.

The Challenge of Incest In Blended Families

One of the greatest challenges in blended, and stepfamilies is incest by stepparents, and between step and half/sibling. As we can see in those biblical families discussed above. And in many cases, it is the stepfathers that are the offenders. According to family experts, incest is more common, and more severe in blended/ stepparent families than is generally reported.

Often, blended families are at a higher risk for step, half/ sibling, and stepparent, sexual abuse; basically, because the natural bonding process at birth between them is not present with these families. The Bible calls this bonding love, natural affection.

Proper Supervision

The lack of proper supervision also contributes to this problem, as new stepparents use older stepsiblings and step/ parents for babysitting options for the younger children far too soon. New couples need to be very, very, careful about leaving stepsiblings, or stepparents, home alone too soon, and in some families, it should not happen at all.

To avoid the risk of stepparent, stepsibling improprieties, it is highly recommended by experts, that the entire family, including the children, receive proper structure, guidance, supervision, and support, early in the marriage; to ensure, healthy transitions, and patterns of communication, and behavior, in the bonding process.

However, God intentionally put these examples of high-profile blended families in the scriptures to also give us hope, that in Him, not only can blended families survive, but all families can survive.

CHAPTER THREE

THE CHALLENGE OF SEXUAL EXPERIENCES THAT PRE-DATE YOUR PRESENT MARRIAGE

One:
It Can Rob You Of The Ability To Have A Trusting Relationship.
Why?

Because, your prior relationships and sexual experiences, are what have developed and shaped, to a great extent, your present relationship, and sexual preferences.

This is true because, the human brain is designed by God to store and recall, all events, and life experiences of the person. Therefore, the mind is the storehouse of everything that we have ever experienced in our lives, waiting to be recalled at the appropriate time. (This process is called, memory, or to remember)

The reward pathway of the brain also controls the natural recall and response, to past rewards and pleasures. The reward pathway of the brain automatically tells, and urges the individual, to repeat a rewarding experience, so that they can get that reward and pleasure again.

The reward pathway of the human brain also tells the memory; to pay particular attention to all details that brought about that rewarding experience, so that it can be repeated, over, and over again in the future.

The natural tendency of the human brain then is to seek to regain and duplicate its greatest pleasure and experience in the present relationship.

The problem is that it can cause your new spouse to feel that they are being compared to your previous relationships, and many times, lead to resistance, suspicion, jealousy, distrust, accusations, arguments, and even abuse. The spirit of jealousy is mentioned in the scriptures. *(Read Num. 5:11-14, 29-31)*

Two:
It Can Also Rob You Of The Ability To Express True Love.
Why is This?

It is true because, sex is the God-given act of expressing true love and intimacy, only in the covenant relationship of marriage. Sex according to God, is the divine act of consummation and bonding of the marriage covenant. *(Read Gen. 2:24, I Cor. 6:16)*

So, if you have given yourself sexually to someone else in that way, you can never give to your new spouse anything that you have not already given to someone else. You can give them sex, but you can never give them the true love that God intended only in the covenant of marriage.

The Challenge Becomes: The frustration of trying to express love in alternative ways. Trying to express love through kind words, gifts, money, and other material things; but pure love can never be expressed through sex because you have given the same intimacy to others.

Three:
It Can Also Rob You Of The Ability To Have A Monogamous Relationship.
What Do I Mean By This?

Because sex is giving your total self to another person, in the most intimate and personal way possible. Sex is a physical, mental, emotional, spiritual, chemical, and social, bonding experience that has a lasting impression and emotional effect.

God said that sex is the act of two people becoming one; sex is to be joined together as in a covenant agreement. Therefore, every sex partner you have ever had is brought into your present relationship experience in some way. **(Again Read Gen. 2:24, I Cor. 6:16)**

The Challenges of This Are: Improper thoughts about other lovers, sexual comparison, guilt, regret, embarrassment, possible interference from former partners, and extended relationships because of children, etc. This can make things very, very difficult.

A Deeper Look Into Stepfamilies

First, we need to accept the fact that, blended/stepfamilies are alternative family units; they are not God's original plan and purpose for the family; and therefore, cannot in these alternative relationships, claim God's original blessings and promises for the family, although you are now saved. Salvation does not exempt or absolve us of past responsibilities and consequences.

Therefore, blended/stepfamilies require a different approach to developing the family structure; and this demands a much greater emotional and social sacrifice, to be successful.

> **Psalm 127:1** *Except the LORD build the house, (family) they labour in vain that build it.*

The Promise Of God To Those In Alternative Marriages

In the book of Jeremiah, God gives an illustration of something that had been designed for a particular purpose but had been damaged to the extent that, it could no longer be restored to its original purpose.

Therefore, it had to be transformed, and redesigned into something entirely different; but still had great value and purpose in the Kingdom of God. I believe that this scripture also speaks of what God can do with a blended family if it is placed in His hands.

> ***Jeremiah 18:1-6*** *The word which came to Jeremiah from the* LORD, *saying, Arise, and go down to the potter's house, and there I will cause thee to hear my words. Then I went down to the potter's house, and, behold, he wrought a work on the wheels. And the vessel that he made of clay was **marred** in the hand of the potter:* **so he made it again another vessel, as seemed good to the potter to make it.** *Then the word of the* LORD *came to me, saying,* **cannot I do with you as this potter?** *saith the* LORD. *Behold, as the clay is in the potter's hand, so are ye in mine hand.*

In this text, I believe that God is giving us a picture of some of our lives by the time we finally come to salvation in Jesus Christ; our lives are so marred, scarred, bruised, and broken by sin, that we have forfeited God's original plan and purpose for our lives.

However, God is still able to salvage us and make something valuable and beautiful out of what is left, if we will trust and obey Him with the second chance that He has given us.

> ***II Timothy 2:21** If a **man** therefore **purge himself** from these, he shall be a **vessel unto honor**, **sanctified** and meet **(fit)** for the **Master's use,** and prepared for every good work. Praise the Lord!*

Blended Families Need Support

According to family experts, if a stepfamily is going to fall apart, it usually happens in the first 2 or 3 years. Therefore, many newly married blended couples need the most help and support immediately.

Unfortunately, most blended couples are either too embarrassed to get help or do not feel the need for help, until it is too late in many cases.

Because of a lack of biblical teaching on blended/step-families, even in most churches, many of these families often struggle alone, isolated from support, help, and the information needed to make good decisions. They are left trying to force fit their families into a nuclear family model, which cannot be done.

This struggle will lead to frustration, disappointment, stress, and anxiety, beyond expectation, and the ability to cope; often leading to another divorce and more brokenness.

Make Parenting Changes and Guidelines Before You Get Married

Couples need to come to an agreement on how they intend to parent together, and then make the necessary adjustments to their parenting styles before they get remarried.

Couples also need to include their children in their discussions and planning; realizing that the children are an important part of the new family dynamics, and they will play a vital role in the health and well-being of the marriage, and the family.

This will make the transition into the blended family much smoother, and the children will not become so easily frustrated, or angry with the new spouse when they make or initiate changes in the home.

Effective Parenting in Blended Families

While newly remarried couples without children can use their early months together, building their own relationship; couples in blended families are often more consumed with their children, and making adjustments to other things, than with each other.

Because, while a first marriage is all about your new partner, the subsequent marriage revolves around the children, and making sure that everyone has a place in the new family dynamics.

First, the couple needs to understand that the first and second marriages are like apples and oranges, and you cannot compare the two. Unfortunately, however, too many couples try to transfer past experiences into their new relationship.

It has been proven with stepfamilies that if the parents try to rush the relationships or force the new family to conform too soon, it could backfire and even make the situation worse.

Now, this is the tough part for the adults: It is important to realize that everyone's role shifts; sometimes drastically when you create a blended family unit.

In fact, when you first bring everyone together, the kids will usually try to figure out, where or even if they belong, in this new family system. If the kids do not feel or believe that they have a place in the family, or if they think that someone is taking their place, they will become resentful and often begin to act out.

CHAPTER FOUR

SEVERAL IMPORTANT AND EFFECTIVE TIPS ON STEP-PARENTING

Let The Bio-Parent Do The Disciplining: This may be a surprise to most couples, but it is true. For stepparents, it is important, early in the marriage, to let the bio-parent do the disciplining.

Even though this might go against everything you believe or what you may have expected, the stepparent needs to allow time to earn the right to take this kind of action.

It is important also that the stepparent, not be the heavy, but they can't just disappear either. However, maintaining their presence, and at the same time, supporting the bio-parent is difficult, but it will be more productive in the long run.

The irony is that, when you relax and support the bio parent, the relationship with your stepchildren will form faster.

The stepparent needs to be a kind of good cop and let the bio-parent be the bad cop if you will! If there is a behavior for which your stepchild needs a consequence, let your spouse deal with it, and support their decision.

The good cop finds out the interests of the stepchild, and develops the relationship, by getting involved in the child's life, based on those discoveries.

Do Not Compete With The Bio-parent

Do not compete with your counterparts; rather, uphold them. In other words, don't try to be a better mom than your stepchild's bio-mom, or a better dad than their bio-dad.

No matter what you think of the bio parent's style of discipline, (or lack thereof) it is important to respect and acknowledge the strength of the biological connection.

This can be very difficult to do when your new spouse is still at war with his or her ex, and possibly, still fighting over the kids and other issues.

Many stepfathers have an attitude, "I'm going to shape up this platoon and lead the troops out of the wilderness." And many stepmoms decide they're going to make up for all the hurt and pain they have endured.

But stepparents are encouraged to establish a relationship with their stepchildren, rather than being a dictator or rigid authoritarians.

Simply be present in the child's life, and avoid fixing things, and people, or competing with the bio-parent.

And no parent, or no one, should ever say anything negative about their ex-spouse, or bio-parent in the presence of the children. They may be your ex-spouse or an ex-relationship, but they will always be your children's mothers and fathers.

Neither should they use their children as pawns or weapons against the bio-parents, no matter how hurt, or angry you may be with them. Your children are not tools or objects, they are children, and they are vulnerable and fragile!

Keep All Parents Involved If Possible!

Children will adjust better to the blended family if they have access to both biological parents. It is important and healthy if all parents are involved and working together toward a parenting partnership; this way, the kids will know that they do not have to choose between their parents.

Let the kids know that you and your ex-spouse will continue to love them and be there for them throughout their lives.

Let the kids know that your new spouse will not be a "replacement" mom or dad, but rather, another person to love and support them. Never, ever, speak ill of an ex-spouse or bio-parent in the presence of the children.

Discover The Interests Of Stepchildren

Discover the things your stepson or stepdaughter likes. Start off as you would with any friendship: find some common ground and do things together that you might both enjoy.

Remember, you are there to build a healthy, appropriate family relationship, not to take the place of your stepchild's mother or father.

You may need to come in as a friend, or a benevolent partner for a while; choosing a role other than a parent, to foster a better family relationship.

The Importance Of One-on-One Time, With Bio-children

Let your spouse have one-on-one time with his or her kids—without you. This can help reduce the displacement and loss that the child might be feeling, and it assures them that they have not been displaced by somebody else.

I know that this flies in the face of the myth of "instant family." However, it has been proven that in a stepfamily, it helps the process of blending the family if each bio-parent is allowed to spend time or do special things with their bio-kids alone; this will help everyone to acclimate and assimilate more easily.

We know that this is where many stepparents get concerned and nervous when their spouse is still spending time with his or her kids alone, and not including them.

Yes, it is true, however, this must be done very carefully, with the intent of bringing the family together, and not continuing in divided relationships. But if you plan to be in this marriage for a while, give it enough time to work itself out; do not worry about it, you will get your turn.

In the meantime, this relieves the bio-parent, releases them to enjoy their children, and assures the stepchildren that you are not there to take their parents away from them.

If this is done with a pure motive, you will be amazed at what it will do for blended families. This reassures the children that they still belong and have not lost the love of their bio-parent to the new spouse.

> **Always Treat Your Stepchildren With Love Even If You Don't Really Feel Love, or Even Like Them Yet.**

Remember, to your stepchildren, you may be seen as the outsider, an intruder. In their minds, you have displaced them or even replaced them.

It is important also to realize that, the pain that some children have experienced, and may continue to experience, after a divorce or break-up of their family, now with a new remarriage and blended family, may cause them to act out.

And, they may not have the skills to talk it out or express their feelings, or what is really going on inside. But the adults need to be patient and give them some time!

Stepparents must understand that you can't make your stepchildren love you, or even like you! It just takes time, hard work, and sacrifice from everyone.

And in many cases, you may feel guilty because you don't love your stepchildren. But the reality is, you may never love them as your own children, or even like them at first. But even if you do not, you can still treat them with love.

There is a definition of love mentioned in the Bible, that is called *"natural affection"* it is the natural love and affection that is unique to biological family members; you will never have that kind of love for your stepchildren.

However, there is another love mentioned in the bible called *"Agape, godly love"* which is the love of God, a benevolent love that you can choose to give.

Therefore, though you may never have a natural affection for your stepchildren, you can have the love of God for them, and therefore, you can treat them the same as your own, though you love them differently.

Remember, true Love is an act, not a feeling. So, treat them in a loving manner; it may surprise you as the relationship develops, and the love you seek may just come along with it.

Fix Yourselves Before You Try to Fix The Children

Many couples will come in for counseling wanting to, "Fix the children." But the truth is, the children are not just broken—the family is broken. So, the question to the adults should always be, are you willing to acknowledge that the pain and brokenness in the family is something that you created, and not the children?

The mistake that many stepparents make is putting the burden of adjustment and change upon the children, rather than themselves, who really caused the problem in the first place.

Do not make your children bear the burden that you should be carrying; it is the parent's responsibility to carry the heaviest load. The parents must be the adults in the marriage, not the children.

If the parents can gain the skills of listening to their children and try to understand what the child is going through over time, the children will usually come around, and respond productively. Always remember, Healing is needed in the entire family!

> ***James 5:16*** *Confess your faults one to another, and pray one for another, that ye **may be healed.** The effectual fervent prayer of a righteous man availeth much.*

As parents, we have the responsibility to listen to the complaints of our children, just as God our Father listens to ours.

> ***Isaiah 1:18*** *Come now, and let us **reason together, saith the** L**ORD:** though your sins be as scarlet, they shall be as white as snow; though they be red like crimson, they shall be as wool.*

***Philippians 4:6-7** Be anxious for nothing, but in **everything by prayer** and supplication, with thanksgiving, **let your requests be made known to God;** [7] and the peace of God, which surpasses all understanding, will guard your hearts and minds through Christ Jesus.*

Children will adjust better to the blended family if they have access to both biological parents. It is important that all parents are involved, and working together toward a parenting partnership that is supportive, and healthy for the children.

CHAPTER FIVE

THE NEED TO UNDERSTAND TRUE LOVE

John 8:32 *And ye shall know the truth, and the truth shall make you free.*

The English word Love is the most misused, misunderstood, and misapplied word in the English language. We say that we love almost everything and everybody. We love our spouse, children, family, friends, pets, houses, cars, clothes, food; our church, our pastors, cities, states, etc.

So you see then, how confusing it can become when someone says, I love you. What do they really mean? How do you love me?

What is the difference between your love for me, and all of those other things, and other people that you said you love? All of these statements are true, but the word "love" in each case really describes a very different experience and expression.

Let us consider the five different types of love mentioned in the Bible that applies to marriage and the family. And don't worry about correctly pronouncing the Greek words used; you will get the meaning of them as we study their meanings going forward.

Here Are The Greek Words and Meanings of The 5 Different Biblical Loves:

(**1**) *"Epithumia"* Attractive Love: (**2**) *"Eros"* Romantic Love: (**3**) *"Storge"* Family Love: (**4**) *"Phileo"* Friendship Love: (**5**) *"Agape"* Divine Love, The Love of God, which is Unconditional, Provisional, Covenant Love.

In This Study, We Will Help Couples Understand Why These Five Different Loves Are Necessary For a Healthy Marriage and Family

FIRST: EPITHUMIA; ATTRACTIVE LOVE

This type of love is typically associated with physical attraction, a strong desire or attraction to someone. In the negative sense, it is called lust, even a feeling of sensuality. Physical desire can be a necessary start, on the way to true love, but not all lustful encounters escalate to levels of true love.

While lust may be necessary to initiate the pursuit of a mate, it is not always followed by the process of falling in love, nor is lust always directed exclusively at the object of a person's love. We see this in the case of King David.

> ***2 Samuel 11:2-3*** *And it came to pass in an evening-tide, that David arose from off his bed, and walked upon the **roof of the king's house**: and from the roof **he saw a woman washing herself**; and **the woman was very beautiful to look upon**. And David sent and **enquired after the woman. (Please Read II Samuel 13:1-15)***

According to psychiatrists, lust can be an altered state of consciousness programmed by the primal urge to mate. Studies suggest that the brain in this phase is much like a brain on drugs.

Also, in the early stage of a relationship, when the sex hormones are raging, lust is fueled by idealization, and projection that is seen, what you hope someone will be or need them to be, rather than seeing the real person, flaws and all.

Because lust is based solely upon physical attraction and fantasy, it often dissipates when the real person surfaces.

And, because this love is emotionally stimulated by physical attraction, it is not sustainable, because aging, and other life issues can cause changes in body composition and appearance.

And this love can begin to diminish, or even cease if the attraction that caused this love is altered, diminished, or eliminated. Therefore, if your marriage is built upon this love, it will not last.

SECOND: EROS; ROMANTIC LOVE

Romantic love: This type of love is intimate, passionate love, sensual or sexual desire. Romantic love is a necessary and important part of our human existence; it was created by God, inspired by God, encouraged, and nurtured by the grace of God.

This love, which is sexual, is also the first commandment given to man by God, because it is His creative design and function for human reproduction to populate the earth, but only in the covenant of marriage.

> *Genesis 1:27-28 So God created man in **his own image, in the image of God** created he him; **male** and **female** created he them. **And God blessed** them, and **God said unto them, Be fruitful, and multiply, and replenish the earth.***

> *Genesis 2:24 Therefore shall **a man** leave his **father** and his **mother,** and shall cleave unto his wife: and **they shall be one flesh. (Read I Corinthians 6:16)***

In males, however, the sex drive is more constant and heavily influenced by visuals, while the female sex drive is more intense and greatly stimulated by romantic words and fictional images.

It's like fishing and bait, women flirt with sex but what they really want is love, and men flirt with love, but what they really want is sex. And lustful men can be very skillful in saying the things that women want to hear and are more likely to get what they want than women, and in too many cases leaving the woman with a child.

However, as romantic, necessary, and sensual as this love is in marriage, because it is also emotionally stimulated, and is based upon the desires of the flesh, it is not sustainable.

And therefore, will begin to fade in about two to four years, if it is not cultivated and nurtured in the marriage.

> ***Proverbs 5:18-19*** *Let your fountain be blessed,* ***and rejoice in the wife of your youth, Let her be as the loving hind and pleasant roe;*** *let her breasts satisfy thee at all times; and be thou ravished always* ***with her love.***

Unfortunately, too many marriages and relationships today are built upon these kinds of loves; and when the attraction, feelings, and thrill are gone, so are they.

THIRD: STORGE; FAMILY LOVE

Familial love: This is the natural instinctive, and affectional love that one has for their family. It is an affectionate love that exists naturally between family members, such as the warm, unforced love shown between spouses, parents, and children, and between siblings.

This love is expected to be such a natural characteristic among family members and humanity, that there was apparently no need to command such love in the New Testament.

The only exception is when people have lost their instinctive affection for their own parents, children, and family, and thus they were said to be: ***"without natural affection."*** *II Timothy 3:3*

This kind of love provides a sense of belonging, comfort, safety, and protection to the family unit. However, because this love is also an emotional or natural love, based upon conditional satisfaction or pleasure in the object of love, it can also fade or diminish because of displeasure, disagreement, and opposition.

The widespread divorce, abortion, and the breakdown of the family are prime examples of this loss of family love and affection in our generation.

*Proverbs 30:11 There is a generation that **curseth their father,** and doth not **bless their mother.***

*II Timothy 3:2-3 For **men shall be lovers of their own selves,** covetous, boasters, proud, blasphemers, disobedient to parents, unthankful, unholy, **Without natural affection.***

*I Timothy 5:8 But if any provide not for his own, and specially for **those of his own house, he hath denied the faith, and is worse than an infidel.***

FOURTH: PHILEO; FRIENDSHIP LOVE

This love is commonly called brotherly love; the kind of love that is based upon friendships, common interests, goals, and personality connection. This love includes loyalty, virtue, equality, familiarity, enjoying activities in common, and mutual forgiveness.

However, a loving friend is important to everyone, because everyone needs someone whom they can trust and be vulnerable with. No one can go through life without at least one close friend, someone that they can rely upon, a person who is trustworthy, someone whom they can be vulnerable with!

A friend that will also hold one another accountable, that can influence, motivate, and encourage one another to grow spiritually, and mature in faith.

This love is also required and is necessary in marriage, and in the family, however, because this love also stems from emotions and a feeling of pleasure, it can, and for many, will diminish in conflict and displeasure. But the scriptures teach us about the attitude and behavior of a true friend.

> ***Proverbs 17:17, 18:24****"A friend loveth at all times" "and there is **a friend that sticks closer than a brother.***

> ***Ephesians 4:26-27, 32*** *Be ye **angry, and sin not**: let not the sun go down **upon your wrath**: Neither **give place to the devil**. And be ye **kind one to another**, **tenderhearted**, **forgiving one another**, even as God for Christ's sake hath forgiven you.*

While all of these loves are important and necessary in marriage, they are not enough to sustain the marriage. However, the love of God is absolutely necessary and is more important than all of the others, because it is the love of God that sustains all others. Now let us consider the Love of God.

FIFTH: AGAPE; DIVINE LOVE, THE LOVE OF GOD

Agape is the highest form of any type of love because it is the love of God; a benevolent, selfless, sacrificial, unconditional, provisional, and covenant love. Agape is not based upon attraction, romance, friendship, or emotions; it is a divine choice to love and care for someone, independent of their response to that love.

Agape love is entirely about the lover, not the one who is loved. It is an act of self-sacrifice, a chosen and deliberate kindness extended to others, even to enemies for whom one has no personal affection.

Agape love, in its purest form, requires no payment or favor in response to its love; it is the covenant love of God.

This is the love that keeps you faithful to your marriage when all of the other natural loves have diminished. This love remains faithful beyond feelings and circumstances.

> ***Romans 5:8*** *But God commendeth his love toward us, in that, while we were yet sinners, Christ died for us.*

> ***Ephesians 5:25, 28 Husbands, love your wives,*** *even as* ***Christ also loved the church,*** *and* ***gave (sacrificed)*** *himself for it. That he might sanctify*

and cleanse it with the washing of water by the word, That he might present it to himself a glorious church, not having spot, or wrinkle, or any such thing; but that it should be holy and without blemish. So ought men to love their wives as their own bodies. He that loveth his wife loveth himself.

What these scriptures are saying to us is that: when the attraction, trust, romance, and thrill are all gone; covenant love will always remain faithful to the covenant of marriage.

<u>The God Kind of Love</u>

This kind of love had never been seen or known until Jesus came and demonstrated it to the world! The people of Jesus' day did not know what to call this kind of love; because at that time there was no name for it. So they coined the Greek phrase, "Agape", The God kind of love.

__I John 3:1__ Behold, what manner of love that the father has bestowed upon us, that we should be called the sons of God.

__John 15:13__ Greater love hath no man than this, that a man __lay down his life for his friends.__

Agape Love Can Only Be Known By What it Does, Not By What it Feels or What it Says.

*I John 4:9-10 In this was made **known the love of God toward us,** because that **God sent His only begotten son** into the world, that we might live through him. Herein is love, not we loved God, but that he loved us, and sent his son to be a propitiation for our sins*

<u>The Way of True Love</u>

In Paul's letter to the Corinthians, he used the word charity to explain the love of God, because charity is the action that makes true love known to others.

*1 **Corinthians 13:4-8** Charity **suffereth long**, and is **kind**; charity **envieth not;** charity **vaunteth not itself,** is **not puffed up**, Doth not behave **itself unseemly**, seeketh not **her own**, is not easily **provoked**, thinketh no **evil;** Rejoiceth not in **iniquity**, but rejoiceth in the truth; **Beareth all things**, believeth all things, hopeth all things, endureth all things. **Charity never faileth.***

1 Corinthians 13:4-8 Gives Us 15 Examples of The Manifestation of True Love, The Love of God:

1. *True Love: "Suffers long and is kind".* Meaning that this love shows kindness even while it is suffering the wrong of others.

2. ***True Love: "Does not envy".*** This love is not jealous or envious of the gifts or accomplishments of others

3. ***True Love: "Boast not itself".*** True love does not boast and brag about itself.

4. ***True Love: "Is not puffed up".*** Is not arrogant or lifted up in self-pride.

5. ***True Love: "Doth not behave itself unseemly".*** Is not rude, and harsh to others.

6. ***True Love: "Seeks not her own".*** True love always seeks the best for others, not itself.

7. ***True Love: "Is not easily provoked".*** True love is not easily irritated or angered.

8. ***True Love: "Thinks no evil".*** True love always thinks and hopes the best in and for others

9. ***True Love: "Rejoice not in iniquity".*** True love takes no pleasure in the wrong, misfortune, or sins in others, and does not keep score of their wrong.

10. ***True Love: "Rejoice in the truth".*** True love rejoices in the truth and goodness of others

11. *True Love: "Beareth all things".* True love always bears the burden and personal responsibility of loving.

12. *True Love: "Believes all things".* True love always believes and expects the best of others.

13. *True Love: "Hopes all things".* True love hopes for the best for others.

14. *True Love: "Endureth all things".* True love never gives up, but always perseveres in love in spite of circumstances.

15. *True Love: "Never fails".* True love never fails to perform its faithful responsibilities and loyal duties of love.

THIS IS THE FAITHFULNESS AND STABILITY THAT ONLY THE LOVE OF GOD CAN PROVIDE!!

CHAPTER SIX

THE NEED FOR A CLEAR VISION FOR YOUR MARRIAGE

The Power of Vision For Your Marriage

Proverbs 29:18 Where there is no vision, the people perish.

Vision is the power and ability to see destiny. And when vision is applied to your future, it creates a mental picture of your future and directs your actions and behavior to accomplish it. Vision serves as a guide to provide a sense of purpose for your life.

The question is, do you know where you want to be in your marriage in the next few years? The answer lies in one simple word: vision.

A couple that is able to define a clear vision for their marriage will find that the disagreements and fighting over key issues are greatly minimized. Having a clear vision places purpose upon your life and your activities.

Without a vision and destination in mind, you would not have a clear and defined path in life. Vision provides this for you. A vision, therefore, ensures that your life goals remain focused when you face adversities and distractions. A vision gives you the reason for your actions, choices, hopes, desires, and dreams.

Vision means mental insight and foresight, the power and ability to envision a goal, and destination for your marriage. When you don't have a clear vision of where you're going, it's impossible to stay on track and stay together.

If you have no idea of your destination, then how do you know where you are going, and when you've arrived? And how would you know when you're on the wrong path? The truth is, you wouldn't know.

When you have a clear vision for your marriage, it brings unity to the marriage. You agree because you both have a clear vision to agree upon. You need to have a vision that brings you together in marriage. Because where there is a vision, you can walk together and stay together.

Amos 3:3 asks the question, "Can two walk together, except they are agreed?"

The answer is no!

Without a vision, there is nothing to keep your life on track, and you will wind up wandering aimlessly through life without purpose and wondering what happened!

Vision is the power to see the future; giving you images

and ideas of what your life can be, dreams and possibilities for your future. Vision is the ability to use your imagination to create dreams and set goals for your life.

A clear vision of God's purpose for your marriage and life also makes suffering and disappointments bearable, because you have divine hope. Vision inspires the depressed and motivates the discouraged to persevere and continue in hope.

As Paul gives us an example, ***Philippians 3:13-14*** *Brethren, I count not myself to have apprehended: but this one thing I do,* ***forgetting those things which are behind,*** *and reaching forth unto* ***those things which are before***, *"I press toward the mark for the prize of the* ***high calling of God in Christ Jesus.***"

> ***I Corinthians 15:58*** *Therefore, my beloved brethren, be ye* ***steadfast, unmovable,*** *always abounding in the work of the Lord, forasmuch as ye know that your* ***labor is not in vain in the Lord.***

THE NEED FOR A WRITTEN LIFE PLAN FOR YOUR MARRIAGE

<u>The Necessity And Importance of Planning Ahead</u>

Habakkuk 2:2 And the LORD *answered me, and said,* **Write the vision**, *and* **make it plain upon tables**, *that he may run (take action) that readeth it.*

Proverbs 14:27 Prepare thy work without, and make it **fit for thyself** *in the field; and* **afterwards** *build thine house.*

Luke 14:28-30 For which of you, intending to build a tower, **sitteth not down first, and counteth the cost,** *whether he have sufficient to finish it? Lest haply, after he hath laid the foundation, and is* **not able to finish it,** *all that behold it begin to mock him, Saying, This man began to build, and was not able to finish.*

What does planning ahead mean to you? Whether your first instinct is to think about marriage, money, or time, the principles behind planning are beneficial for every area of your life.

Planning ahead is bringing the future into the present so that you can do something about it now. When planning is done right, it will help you to be more effective in accomplishing new objectives and reaching your life goals.

The problem is, most people spend more time planning for their wedding than planning for their marriage; or spend more time planning for a one-week vacation, than for their family and for their life together.

In other words, most people wander aimlessly through life, from week to week, with no clear plan or destination in mind, and then are surprised when life does not turn out the way they wanted it to.

Planning ahead means less worrying about what will happen tomorrow, or next week because you will be in charge of your own time, money, and destiny. This means that you will be able to spend your time and your resources more effectively.

Leaving things until the last minute will always cost you more! It can cost you more time, more money, and most importantly, more frustration!

Sometimes, a little planning can go a long way! If you prepare for the challenges ahead of time, then you will not feel like you are running around trying to catch up or trying to fix something that did not have to be broken in the first place!

The fact is that planning ahead will always make you more productive in your day-to-day activities. Having a clear action plan will always allow you to get more done in less time. For this reason, I believe that everyone—especially married couples, should take the time to create a clear, written, goal and plan for their marriage and for their lives.

Why A Life Plan Is Needed In Marriage

1. **A life plan helps you to learn how to communicate and come to an agreement about your lives together.**

2. **A life plan will help you clarify your most important priorities.**

3. **A life plan will enable you to maintain balance in your lives.**

4. **A life plan will provide a filter, by which you can say "no" to less important things.**

5. **A life plan will empower you to identify and address your current realities.**

6. **A life plan will equip you to envision a better future for yourselves.**

7. **A life plan will serve as a road map for accomplishing what matters most to you.**

8. **A life plan will help to ensure that you do not finish life with regrets.**

For first-time planners, I usually recommend a one-year plan; that way, your goals will seem reachable, keeping you encouraged and motivated. I also recommend revisiting your progress, every two or three months, to make sure that you are on schedule.

This will allow you the opportunity to recalibrate early if necessary. I call these revisits joy junctions because they allow you to see and enjoy your progress and success and encourage you to keep going.

My suggestion also for all couples: When you have completed your budget and life plans; lay them before the Lord, and pray over them, for His guidance and blessings; and make a covenant vow to God that you will follow through, with every agreement. And always remember, you are planning your marriage, your future. and your life!

Write The Life Plan For Your Marriage

> **A Goal is Where You Want to Go: A Plan is How You're Going to Get There**

Your Plan Must Be: Specific - Measurable – Attainable – Realistic -Timely

Specific: Specific goals are easier to follow and have a much greater chance of being accomplished than general goals. There must be specific reasons, purpose, and benefits, in accomplishing the goal.

EXAMPLE: A general goal would be, "To get in shape." But a specific goal would say, "To Join a health club and workout for 3 days a week." That is specific!

Measurable: Establish concrete criteria for measuring progress toward the attainment of each goal you set. If your goals are not measurable, you have no way of knowing if you are making progress.

When you can measure your progress, you can see your success, and feel a sense of accomplishment. This helps you to stay focused and stay the course.

Attainable: Your goals must be important enough to you, that it causes you to begin to figure out a plan to get you there. If goals are attainable, you can and will develop the attitudes, abilities, skills, and financial capacity to reach them. Unattainable goals will only serve to cause frustration and anxiety for you.

Realistic: To be realistic, a goal must represent an objective toward which you are both willing and able to achieve. A goal can be both high and yet realistic; you are the only one who can decide just how high your goals should be, and how hard you are willing to work at attaining them. But be sure that the goal is one that you can realistically achieve. Plan the work and work the plan!

Timely: Do not procrastinate; a goal should be grounded within a time frame. Without a time, frame, there is no sense of urgency. For instance, if you want to lose 10 lbs. when do you want to lose it? "Someday" is not good enough. But if your goals are anchored within a time frame, then you have set your subconscious mind in motion to begin working to achieve them.

A time frame makes your goals tangible; you can experience them with your senses. When your goals and plans are tangible, you are making them specific, measurable, and thus attainable. That is the ultimate goal of making plans!

ABOUT THE AUTHOR

Dr. John Davis

Dr. John Davis is the founder and former Pastor of Bethesda Word of Faith Church, and Bethesda Outreach Ministries, in Sarasota, Florida. He currently serves in ministry at International Praise Church of God (Elgin, SC). Dr. Davis has a Bachelor of Theology from International Theological Seminary of Bradenton Florida; a Bachelor of Theology, Master of art in Ministry, and Doctor of Theology from International College of Ministry of Orlando, Florida. Dr. Davis is also the Founder/President and CEO of Bethesda Theological Seminary, a professor, preacher, and author.

www.ingramcontent.com/pod-product-compliance
Lightning Source LLC
Chambersburg PA
CBHW040158160726
48006CB00014B/1799